The Big Goal

What's Your Goal?

Sloane Gould

SOCIAL AND EMOTIONAL LEARNING FOR THE REAL WORLD™

Rosen Classroom™

I have a goal.

I want to climb.

I climb up the rope.

I climb up the wall.

I climb up the rocks.

I climb up high.

Words to Know

rocks

rope

wall